THE BEAST

By Donald Peart

September 2022 Edition

ISBN: 978-0-9702301-1-9

Table of Contents

Foreword --1

The Beasts --3

The Leopard Beast --5

The Name of the Beast --7

Blasphemous Names --10

The Number of the Beast --14

The Image of the Beast --17

The Worship of the Beast --19

The Mark of the Beast --21

Marked by Thoughts --23

Marked by Technology --25

No Desire for Women --28

False Prophets and the Beast --32

The Righteousness of Jesus --36

The Sea of Glass for Priests --40

The Harvest --44

Afterword, the Eight King --47

Table of Contents

Foreword

One of the responsibilities of the Church is to demonstrate the righteous acts of Jesus Christ to the world (religious orders, social orders, governmental orders, business orders, hurtful spiritual orders, etc.), to manifest to them the righteousness of Jesus Christ, the Lamb of God. The righteousness of Jesus, if accepted, that causes some in the world to become victorious (overcomers) out of the beast, out of the beast's name, out-of-the number of the beast, and out of the image of the beast.

In the book of the Revelation of Jesus Christ, the Lord Jesus made it clear that the systems of men are but "beasts," though it may appear as beautiful metals[1] to some. And, according to the book of Revelation, the manifestation of the Lamb of God righteous-acts empowers people to become victorious "out-of" the beast. Also, in my list above of things of the beast that can be overcome ("the beast, the beast's name, the number of the beast, and image of the beast), "the mark of the beast" and worshipping the image of the beast appears to be excluded. That is, it appears that after a person takes the mark of the beast, or giving oneself the mark of the beast, and worshipping of the beast, victory out of the "mark of the beast" and out of the worship of the beast may not be attainable. This appears to be borne out in Revelation 20:4, relative to the first resurrection.

1

Revelation 14:9-11: [9]Then another angel, a third one, followed them, saying with a loud voice, "If anyone worships the beast and his image and receives a mark on his forehead or his hand, [10]he also will drink of the wine of the wrath of God …. [11]"… they have no rest day and night, those who worship the beast and his image, and whoever receives the mark of his name."

*Revelation 20:4: Then I saw … those who **had not** worshiped the beast or his image and **had not** received the mark on their forehead and their hand; and they came to life and reigned with Christ for a thousand years.*

Hence, the warning from an angel, or messenger ("a third angel") declaring what can happen if a person takes on the mark of the beast and if a person worships the beast. **Yet, this book intends to show that victory out of the beast is possible and does occur;** and the righteous-acts of the Lamb of God is listed as a source of deliverance from the beast and its systems!

With that said, the first few chapters are defining chapters, providing a definition of the beast and its' order.

The Beasts

Who or what is the beast? Does the beast exist in every age? Or a better question is: does a beast exist now?

What or who are beasts?

1. A beast is defined as a ruling kingdom or king (a ruler of that beast-like kingdom), in a given generation, that has the heart of a beast[2]. Note: Jesus called King Herod a "fox,"[3] which is a beast
2. Hence, beasts are defined as a person and/or a kingdom that has the characteristics of a beast.
3. In the Bible, the prophet Daniel define "four[4] great beasts" as "kings" and "kingdom"[5]
4. The first kingdom identified as a beast was Babylon (modern-day Iraq).
5. The second beast Kingdom is Medes and Persia (modern-day Iran).
6. The third beast kingdom was Greece, started by Alexander, the great.
7. The fourth kingdom is a diversified iron kingdom, to include, but not limited to the Roman empire and all the Greco-Roman kingdoms that followed until God's Stone Kingdom replaces all the former four (4)[6] kingdoms.

Does a beast exist in every age?

1. A beast system does exist in every age. Daniel declared that there would be **only** four (4) beast

kingdoms before a fifth (5th) kingdom (the fifth Kingdom is the Kingdom of God established).[7]
2. Therefore, until Jesus sets up his Kingdom, beast kingdoms (one of the four, or all four beast spirits), still exist and still rules in the system of men.

Does a beast exist now?

1. According to the beloved apostle John, a beast, with its' sixth head or king, existed in his days,[8] with other beasts to follow.
2. In Revelation 17, John saw a seven-headed beast. An angel said to John, of the seven-headed beast he saw, "there are seven kings: five are fallen, **and one is,** and the other has not come as yet." Revelation 17:11 also calls the eight head of the beast, a beast. Thus, the heads or the kings are all beasts. [9]
3. Beast kingdoms will exist[10] as four (4) forms[11] until the God of heaven "rises" His Kingdom, the fifth (5th)[12] Kingdom that has no end.

The Leopard Beast

In Revelation, chapter 13, the beast is described as a leopard, with a lion's mouth and bear's feet. If one is to interpret this description of this beast according to the Scriptures, an interpretation is as follows.

1. According to the prophet Daniel,[13] throughout the book of Daniel, the leopard represents the kingdom of Greece or the principles of the Greek's form of government and imperialism. The lion's mouth can represent Babylonian[14] principles that devour. The bear's feet can represent the cruelty of Persia (modern-day Iran).

2. According to the prophet Hosea,[15] the leopard represents a beast kingdom that observes its citizen (we can call this spying to control and devour), the bear represents cruelty that tears the heart, while the lion represents governments of men devouring humanity with "none to rescue" the ones being devoured.

3. The leopard beast can also represent the adaptation of governmental principles and social principles of the Greeks, or the ruling of the "spirit of Greece"[16] in the government of men; or the ruling again of the "prince [spirit] of Greece"[17] that ruled over the Greeks and ruled in Alexander, the great. This appears to be the same Greek spirit that also ruled over the four (4) division of Alexander's kingdom after his death.

4. The leopard beast also represents the governmental principles, social beliefs, spiritual beliefs, militaristic principles, imperialist principles, etcetera, of the Greeks.

With that said, I was in a season of fasting in 1992. It was about the 9th day of the fast, and it was my first fast going beyond 3 days. My body was without strength; and as I rested on the sofa while my beloved Judith fixed me some soup; I came to be in a trance[18] and heard a voice say, **"The way is being made for the spirit of Greece."** I then heard a voice say, "A great tragedy shall happen in America," as I heard the voice speak, I saw president Bush standing upon a pile of rubble exactly as President Bush did after 9/11. I then heard the voice say, "After the tragedy, I will bring forth the Boy Scouts."

The way is being made for the spirit of Greece, also called the invisible "prince of Greece," also called the leopard beast.

The Name of the Beast

So many people have tried to tag some American presidents as being the beast, by using their names to tally up 666. That is because some presidents' first name has six letters, and their middle name has six letters and their last name has six letters, then some have erroneously concluded that that particular president has the number of the beast linked to their names.

The Scripture is clear what the beast's name is. **The name of the beast is blasphemy.**

*Revelation 13:1: And I stood upon the sand of the sea and saw a beast ... and upon his heads the **name of blasphemy.***

*Revelation 13:1b, NAS: Then I saw a beast ... and on his head were **blasphemous names.***

*Revelation 17:3: And he carried me away in the Spirit into a wilderness; and I saw a woman sitting on a **scarlet beast, full of blasphemous names,** having seven heads and ten horns.*

It is clear from the Scriptures above that the "name" of the beast is "blasphemy," or he has "blasphemous names." In other words, nothing but blasphemy, in every form, is the "name" (nature, character, or what he is called by) of this beast. Here are some samples of his blasphemy (evil-speaking, or defaming people).

*Revelation 13:5a: And there was given unto him a mouth speaking great things and **blasphemies** ....*

*Revelation 13:6: And he opened his mouth in **blasphemy** against **God**, to **blaspheme** his **name**, and his **tabernacle**, and **them that dwell in heaven**.*

It is very clear from the references above, that the beast does nothing but blaspheme; hence, his name being blasphemy. The beast blasphemed against God; the beast blasphemed God's name. The beast blasphemed God's tabernacle. The beast blasphemes those who dwell in heaven. With that said, the ultimate and only unforgivable blasphemy is to say that the Holy Spirit who was in Jesus is satanic or unclean. That is, as the religious leaders in Jesus' days blasphemed the Holy Spirit, calling the Holy Spirit who was in Jesus "unclean;" so it appears that the beast will blaspheme the Holy Spirit in the Saints. That is, the beast will propagate that the true Disciples of Jesus Christ is evil or unclean because of our biblical beliefs that are contrary to the beliefs of the beast's order.

Mark 3:22-30: [22]And the scribes which came down from Jerusalem said, He has Beelzebub, and by the prince of the 'demons' casts he out 'demons.' [23]And he called them unto him, and said unto them in parables, How can Satan cast out Satan? [24]And if a kingdom is divided against itself, that kingdom cannot stand.[25]And if a house is divided against itself, that house cannot stand. [26]And if Satan rises against himself, and be divided, he cannot stand, but has an end. [27]No man can enter into a strong man's house, and spoil his goods, except he will first bind the strong man; and then he will spoil his house. [28]I say unto you, All sins shall be forgiven unto the sons of men, and blasphemies 'as-much-as" they shall blaspheme: *29But he that shall* **blaspheme against the Holy 'Spirit'** *has not forgiveness, 'into the age' but is in danger of eternal damnation: 30*__Because they said, He hath an unclean spirit.__

The narrative above defines a type of blasphemy that will not be forgiven. The unforgivable blasphemy is to call the Holy Spirit, who was in Jesus, an unclean spirit. That is, blasphemy is to call something opposite its true nature (Revelation 2:9). Again, the beast blasphemed God, God's name, God's tabernacle; and all who dwell in God's heaven. One facet of the beast's blasphemy is to call the Holy God, His tabernacle and God's holy people unclean. Thus, it appears that the beast committed and will commit the unforgivable blasphemy. Here is proof that the beast was not forgiven his blasphemy. The beast will be eventually cast into the lake of fire, "the Second Death" — a death that is into the ages of the ages,

Revelation 19:20: And the **beast** *was taken, and with him the false prophet that 'produced' miracles before him, with which he deceived them that had received the mark of the beast, and them that worshipped his image.* **These both were cast alive into a lake of fire burning with brimstone.**

Revelation 20:10: And the devil who deceived them was thrown into **the lake of fire and brimstone,** *where the beast and the false prophet are also; and they will be tormented day and night* **forever and ever.**

Revelation 20:14: Then Death and Hades were thrown into the lake of fire. **This is the second death, the lake of fire.**

Blasphemous Names

There are two types of blasphemies. There is a blasphemy that can be forgiven. There is blasphemy that will not be forgiven; blasphemy that causes the blasphemer to not "hold-in" forgiveness; instead, they "hold-in" eternal sin or eternal judgment. The beast appears to function in a blasphemy that will not be forgiven. This is demonstrated in his final judgment, as referenced in the previous chapter. With that said, let us first prove that there is blasphemy that can be forgiven.

Mark 3:28-29: *28I say unto you, **All sins shall be forgiven unto the sons of men, and blasphemies 'as-much-as" they shall blaspheme:** 29But he that shall blaspheme against the Holy 'Spirit' has not forgiveness, 'into the age' but is in danger of eternal damnation.*

Jesus indicated in the reference above that all sins and blasphemes **"shall be forgiven."** This promise was fulfilled in one of the great apostles, Paul. Paul stated that he was a "blasphemer;" yet, he received mercy and forgiveness.

1 Timothy 1:12-14: *12And I thank Christ Jesus our Lord, who hath enabled me, for that he counted me faithful, putting me into the ministry; 13Who was before **a blasphemer,** and a persecutor, and injurious: **but I obtained mercy** because I did it ignorantly in unbelief. 14And the grace of our Lord was exceeding abundant with faith and love which is in Christ Jesus.*

Paul made it clear he was a blasphemer; however, he obtained mercy and forgiveness. My point in reviewing this is that some may have walked in the name of the beast—blasphemy. However, they may not have done the unforgivable blasphemy; and therefore, they can be delivered out of the name of the beast.[19] This deliverance through mercy and forgiveness is linked to blasphemers repenting. If there is **no repentance**, there can be no forgiveness.

Revelation 16:8-9: *[8]And the fourth angel poured out his vial upon the sun, and power was given unto him to scorch men with fire. [9]And men were scorched with great heat, and **blasphemed** the name of God, which hath power over these plagues: and **they repented not** to give him glory.*

Revelation 16:10-11: *[10]And the fifth angel poured out his vial upon the seat of the beast, and his kingdom was full of darkness, and they gnawed their tongues for pain, [11]And **blasphemed the God** of heaven because of their pains and their sores, and **repented not** of their deeds.*

It is clear from the references above that the purpose of the plagues is to encourage repentance. Instead, they blasphemed God. Besides, the fact that they blasphemed God, showed that they had the name of the beast in their foreheads (their thoughts manifested through their words). Yet, if they had repented, God would have forgiven them as he forgave Paul, who became one of the greatest apostles who ever lived. If God did not want to forgive them, it would not have been stated that they did not repent of their deeds.

The second form of blasphemy is the blasphemy that will not be forgiven. The blasphemy that cannot be forgiven, is to blaspheme against the Holy Spirit. As indicated in the previous Chapter, and as referenced below, Jesus defines this kind of blasphemy as calling the Holy Spirit an unclean spirit. That is, if one reads the context of Mark, chapter 3, the Scribes insinuated that the Spirit that was in Jesus was Beelzebub (Satan). Jesus shocked them with His response to their blasphemy, by letting them know that they committed an unpardonable blasphemy.

Mark 3:29-30: [29]*But he that shall* **blaspheme against the Holy 'Spirit not hold'** *forgiveness, 'into the age' but is 'holding-in' eternal damnation.*[1] [30]***Because they said, He has an unclean spirit.***

The beast must have practiced this type of unpardonable blasphemy because the beast and the false prophet, with Satan following them to the same place a thousand years afterward, were all cast into the Lake of Fire, the Second Death. According to Jesus, blasphemy must have caused them to forfeit the ability to hold forgiveness. Instead, they "held-in eternal sin." Thus, any who adopt the name

---

[1] Some translations read "eternal sin"

of the beast to the ultimate place of blaspheming the Holy Spirit, will "hold-in eternal judgment."

Revelation 19:20: And the **beast** *was taken, and with him the false prophet that 'produced' miracles before him, with which he deceived them that had received the mark of the beast, and them that worshipped his image.* **These both were cast alive into a lake of fire burning with brimstone.**

Revelation 20:14: And death and hell were cast into **the lake of fire. This is the second death.**

Yet, some like the great apostle Paul will repent of blasphemy; and they will be delivered out of the beast. Saying, yet it another way, Jesus will forgive blasphemy to those who repent, if they have not blasphemed the "'Clean' Spirit."

Revelation 15:2: And I saw as it were a sea of glass mingled with fire: and them that had gotten the victory **out-of**-*the beast, and* **'out-of'** *his image, and* **'out-of'** *his mark, and* **'out-of'** *the number of his name, stand on the sea of glass, having the harps of God.*

The Number of the Beast

Six-six-six (666) has become a notorious number that symbolizes the Devil and evil people. However, it has a broader meaning than just the Devil or evil men. According to the Scriptures, six-six-six (666) is a number **"because"** of man. It is not the number of "man," but the number **"because"** of man. Thus, there is a broader meaning of six-six-six (666).

*Revelation 13:18: Here is wisdom. Let him that hath understanding count **the number of the beast:** for it is the number of a man, and his number is Six hundred threescore and six.*

We see above that six-six-six (666) is the "number of the beast." The verse continues to say that the number of the beast "is the number **of** 'man.'" However, the word **"of"** is a translation of the Greek word **"gar,"** which means **"because,"** or "cause" (as in causation), **"assigning a reason."**[20] **"Because of-man it-is"**

The reason why number 666 exists is **"because of"** man, or man is the "reason" why the number exists, and this number is "the number **of** the beast." In this phrase, "of" is the translation of the genitive case of the Greek word "tou," which is translated as "of-the." Thus, the beast is the "source" or "possessor" of the number 666.

Man is the cause for the number of the beast. This number will be placed on the right hand (what people does with their hands) and on the forehead (changing how people see and think). With that said, here is a question. Is the number of the beast (666) physical or spiritual? **The answer is, yes!**

Yes, it may one day be written physically in humans, or it is indeed also a spiritual number written in one's hands and mind; meaning, the number is manifested in the character of one's mind and the character of what one does with his/her hands. Or it may be linked to **"technology"**[21] being used "on" and "in" humans.

I will also say this, the number of the beast (666) is related to commerce, or marketing, or merchandising. *"... No man might buy or sell, 'if not' he that had the mark, or the name of the beast, or the number of his name. Here is wisdom. Let him that has understanding count the number of the beast: for it is the number 'because of man;' and his number is six hundred 'sixty' and six (Revelation 13:17-18).*

There will come a time and now is to a degree when the only way to buy or sell will be to hold or have the currency of the beast. There are three ways the inhabitants of the earth will be able to buy and sell. Some must have the blasphemous name or nature of the beast in their forehead (minds) or on their hands. Some must have the mark (character) of the beast on their forehead

15

(mind or perspective) or their hands. Some must also have the number of the beast written on their forehead (mind) or their hands.

With that said, what does the number of the beast represents? Here is one way of determining the representation of 666. There is the **name** of the beast. There is the mark of the beast's **name**. There is the number of the beast's **name**.

- The beast's name[22]
- Mark of his name[23]
- Number of his name[24]

The common denominator of all of the above is "**name.**" We have learned that the **name** of the beast is **blasphemy.** Hence, the **mark** of the beast's name is the mark **of the beast's blasphemy.** The **number** that represents the beast's blasphemy is the number 666. Yes, **666 is the number that represents beast-like blasphemy against God, not necessarily Satan.**

The Image of the Beast

An image can represent a manmade idolatrous copy of something they have seen in their minds, as well as an image can be a person replicating someone invisible by the lifestyle he/she lives.

Jesus is the "image of the invisible God."[25] Thus, Jesus is the "icon" of God. Jesus is the "likeness" of God. Jesus is the "simulation" of God. Jesus "resembled" God. Jesus said he who seen Him (Jesus) have seen the heavenly Father.[26]

Revelation 13:14 states that some in the earth would "make an image **to** the beast." Hence, people will "simulate" the beast. Some will walk in the "likeness" of the beast. Some will "resemble" the spirit in the beast. In other words, the making of an image to the beast also has a spiritual mimicking application.

"Making an image to the beast" may also represent an idolatrous image. In other words, there will come a time when a "copy" of the beast will be made; and according to the Scriptures, the false prophet, "another beast," will give "spirit" unto the image of the beast that will cause the image of the beast both to speak and to cause the death of those who refuse to worship the speaking image.[27]

Thus, the image of the beast is both humankind mimicking the beast in their lifestyles; and/or a literal image of the beast being made for the express purpose of forcing beast worship (governmentally and socially). One of the signs of beast worship is to worship its military capabilities to make war! And there will come a time when the beast system uses the military against Christians—State-sponsored persecution against Jesus' disciples.

*Revelation 12:17: So, the dragon was enraged with the woman, and **went off to make war** with the rest of **her 'seed,'** who keep the commandments of God and hold to the testimony of Jesus.*

*Revelation 13:4: they **worshiped the dragon** because he gave his authority to the beast; and **they worshiped the beast,** saying, "Who is like the beast, and who can **wage war** with him?"*

*Revelation 13:7: It was also **given to him to make war** with the **saints and to overcome them,** and authority over every tribe and people and tongue and nation were given to him.*

The Worship of the Beast

Mankind was created to worship the one (1) and only true God, the God of our Lord Jesus Christ; the God of the Church; the same God of Israel. However, we can see throughout history, and even in this age, man has worshipped other gods and is worshipping other gods.

The first sayings of God to Moses and Israel is: *"you shall not have any other gods before me .... You shall not worship them or serve them; for I the Lord your God am a jealous God."* [28] God says those who worship any gods other than the God of Jesus Christ, "hates"[29] the God of Jesus. Yes, all who serve, and worship man-made idols shows that they "hate" God. They may publicly deny that they hate God; however, their action of worshipping idols indicates differently.

In the book of Revelation, we learn that beast worship or the worship of the beast will eventually become mandatory with a death penalty[30] for all who don't worship the beast's image. Only those whose names that **are written** in the Lamb's Book of Life **will not**[31] worship the beast. Saying it another way, only those who keep the "faith of-Jesus"[32] to the point of dying for the Lord, will show themselves as not being worshipers the beast. We are commanded not to worship any idols and any demons[33] behind the idols. Shortly, as it is now in some nations, the spirit-demons behind the diols will be speaking to some more openly; and some nations will eventually adopt the death penalty for not worshipping their idols.

Revelation 13:14-15: ¹⁴*And* **["another beast"]** *deceives them that dwell on the earth by those* **'signs'** *which he had* **'authority'** *to do in the sight of the beast; saying to them that dwell on the earth, that they should make an image* **to** *the beast, which had the wound by a sword, and did live.* ¹⁵*And he* **'was given'** *to give* **'spirit'** *unto the image of the beast, that the image of the beast should both speak, and cause that as many as would not worship the image of the beast* **should be killed.**

Revelation 9:20: The rest of mankind, who were not killed by these plagues, **did not repent** *of the works of their hands,* **so as not to worship demons, and the idols of gold and of silver and of brass and of stone and of wood,** *which can neither see nor hear nor walk.*

The Mark of the Beast

Revelation 15:2 (in all the Greek texts, except for two), and Revelation 20:4, implies that there may be no victory out of the "mark of the beast," for those who receive the mark of the beast, and apparently no victory out of the worship of the beast's image, for those who worships the image of the beast.

The Greek word used for "mark"[34] used in the phrase "mark of the beast" is akin to the word "character."[35] "Mark" is used eight (8)[2] or nine (9) times in the Bible, and "character" is used once.

"Character" is **only** used of Jesus, the Christ, and is translated as "expressed image" (an image that is pressed), "exact representation," "exact imprint," "exact expression." Philo used it as the character of the mind. 2 Maccabees 4:10 defines it as "way of life." With that said,, Jesus, the Christ, the Son of the Living God, is the exact image of God, His Father, who is also the heavenly Father of those who believes that Jesus is "the Christ." It follows that the word "mark" used for the mark of the beast is used seven (7) times in the book of Revelation and once (1) in the book of Acts, for a total of eight (8) times.

In Acts 17:29, in various translations, the Greek word for "mark" ("charagma") is translated or defined as "an

---

[2] Majority Texts and Alexandrian Texts omit the "mark" in Revelation 15.

image formed," "image made," "graven," and an "image fashioned." Therefore, one can conclude that the "mark" of the beast is "an image formed" of the beast. If the Greek word for mark ("charagma") is akin to the Greek word "character", then the mark of the beast is the **"characteristic"** of the beast.

The mark of the beast is the "formed image" of the beast in the character of people; and apparently, this mark <u>may be</u> irreversible. That is when Revelation 15:2 declared those who were **victorious "out-of"** things related to the beast, "the mark of the beast" and "beast's worship" were excluded. Revelation 15:2, indicates that victory out of the beast, victory out of the beast's image, victory out of the number of the beast's name could be accomplished.

With that said, because Revelation 15:2 states the phrase "victory out-of-the beast" (in general terms); and considering God's "mercy" to be potentially for "all,"[36] maybe, the phrase "victory out-of-the beast" may allow for victory out of the mark of the beast and the worship of the beast, depending on whether they gave themselves[3] the mark of the beast, or if they actively participated in receiving/taking[4] the mark of the beast? I am not sure? **Only, God knows!**

---

[3] Revelation 13:16
[4] Revelation 14:9; 14:11; Revelation 20:4

Marked by Thoughts

The mark of the beast is propagated by false prophets and can also be imparted through false prophets. The mark of the beast is also caused by technology. The mark of the beast is also caused by man's internal passion or internal anger. With that said, in this section, my focus is the mark of the beast that is caused by "thoughts," or "internal-passion."

*Acts 17:29, NASB: Being then the children of God, we ought not to think that the Divine Nature is like gold or silver or stone, **an image formed** by the **art** and **thought** of man.*

As a reminder, the phrase "an image formed" is the same word translated as "mark" (of the beast) in the book of Revelation.

"Art" is "technes" the root word for technology, technician, technical, tech, craft, craftsman (tradesman), and so on. "Thought" is a Greek compound "in-thumos," meaning in-passion, in-anger, in-sacrifice-anger, in-kill-anger, in-lust, and so on.

Hence, Acts 19:29 could read: *"Being then the children of God, we ought not to think that the Divine Nature is like gold or silver or stone, **'marked'** by the **'tech'** and **'in-kill-anger'** of man.*

The thought here (no pun intended) is that mankind can be marked with beastly nature through their internal-anger-thoughts, and by technology (especially

23

technology that is used for evil or conveys evil). The word for "thought" used in Acts 19:29c, relating to "mark" is used four (4) places[37] in the Bible; and implies evil thought and blasphemous thoughts. The point that is being made is that the mark or character of the beast can be permanently engraved in people through evil and blasphemous thoughts.

Saying it another way, the beast, energized by Satan, and the false prophet, "another beast," also a part of the 'corporate Satan, will corrupt the thoughts of some to the point of **"marking"** them with the beast's blasphemy against God, the beast's blasphemy against Jesus, the beast's blasphemy against Jesus' disciples, and so on.

*Matthew 9:4, NASB: And Jesus knowing their **in-kill-anger'** said, "Why are you thinking evil in your hearts?"*

*Acts 17:29, NASB: Being then the children of God, we ought not to think that the Divine Nature is like gold or silver or stone, **'marked'** by the **'tech'** and **'in-kill-anger'** of man.*

Marked by Technology

The mark of the beast is also caused by technology.

*Acts 17:29, NASB: Being then the children of God, we ought not to think that the Divine Nature is like gold or silver or stone, **an image formed** by the **art** and thought **of man.***

As a reminder, the phrase "an image formed" is the same word translated as "mark" (of the beast) in the book of Revelation.

"Art" is "technes" the root word for tech, technology, technician, technical, craft, craftsman (tradesman), and so on.

"Technes" (craft) is used both negative (Acts 17:29) and positive Acts 18:3. In a positive sense, it is used of the tent-making trade. In Acts 17:29 it is used negatively of "art" of idolatry. The same is true for technology today. It can be used for positive outcomes, or it can be used for negative outcomes.

The mark of the beast will be in the forehead and hands of those who accept the mark. What does this mean relative to technology? Does this mark of technology relate to chips being inserted into human hands; and eventually, incorporated into the forehead (the eyes or minds of humans)? This is possible.

Remember, Revelation, chapter 13 indicated that no one will be able to buy or sell without the mark of the beast in their forehead or their hand. As we learned in the previous chapter, the mark can be imparted or implemented through internal-anger, or through tech, as we are reviewing again.

Daniel, chapter 2, states that the "iron" kingdom will attempt to "mingle with "clay" (the seed of men). This may mean that humanity will be mixing tech (iron-related items) in the body (brain, eyes, hands, feet, etc.) of mankind.

Technology can also mark humans just by using some of the available technology applications of today. Think about it! Some cannot take a break from a cell phone, tablets, PCs, etc. Why? Technology is addictive and it marks the mind to crave for more and more and more …

Thus, there may come a time when the mark of the beast (technology in humans) will carry the currency of trade (buying and selling).

Revelation 13:16-17, NASB: [16]*And he causes all, the small and the great, and the rich and the poor, and the freemen and the slaves, to be given a mark on their right hand or their forehead,* [17]*and [he provides]that no one will be able to buy or to sell, except the one who has* **the mark,** *[either]* **the name of the beast** *or* **the number of his name**

What will you do if the mark of the beast is offered to you? Have you given that possibility thought? Will you do as the "voice from heaven" recommends?

Revelation 14: 9-13, NASB: ⁹Then another angel, a third one, followed them, saying with a loud voice, "If anyone worships the beast and his image and receives a mark on his forehead or his hand, ¹⁰he also will drink of the wine of the wrath of God, which is mixed in full strength in the cup of His anger; and he will be tormented with fire and brimstone in the presence of the holy angels and the presence of the Lamb. ¹¹"And the smoke of their torment goes up forever and ever; they have no rest day and night, those who worship the beast and his image, and whoever receives the mark of his name." ¹²Here is the perseverance of the saints who keep the commandments of God and their faith in Jesus. ¹³And I heard a voice from heaven, saying, "Write, 'Blessed are the dead who die in the Lord from now on!'" "Yes," says the Spirit, "so that they may rest from their labors, for their deeds follow with them."

Are you willing **not** to receive the mark of the beast, even if it means death? Are you willing to resist the worship of the beast, even if it means death as Shadrach, Meshach and Abed-nego?[38] According to the Holy Scriptures, those whose names are written in the Book of Life, through our Lord Jesus Christ, will not accept or take-on anything that relates to the beast, his name, his mark, his worship, his image, his number!

No Desire for Women

In the book of Daniel, one of the four kings that ruled (after the division of Alexander, the great, kingdom into four kingdoms[39]), prefigures the beast to come; and he also prefigures the "man of lawlessness or the man of sin."[40] In the book of Daniel 11:37, we learn that a king, a man, **"show no regard ... for the desire for women."** This statement may seem casual; however, this statement has serious implications.

That is, it appears that the beast, who is also called a king,[41] maybe a homosexual.[42] The Scripture also implies that the beast will be recruiting homosexual and lesbians to fight against the Lamb of God and those who follow the Lamb of God. Thus, the difficult topic of proper sexuality should not be avoided. So, let us take a look at same-sex as it relates to the beast.

The beast is a worshipper of Satan. According to the Scriptures,[43] Satan only gives authority and power to those who worship Satan. The Scriptures also teaches that when a creature (a created being) worship (creature (another created being), it is defined as "the lie."[44] "The lie" or "creature worshipping creature" results in same sexuality, "female with a female" and "men 'in' men."

That is the mirror practices of worshiping a created being is demonstrated is sexual practices. You see created being worshiping created being instead of created beings worshipping the Creator is wrong and is the same as, or

28

results in, homosexual or lesbian practice. In other words, the same gender sexuality is a result of created being worshiping another created being. Created beings (creation) are supposed to worship the Creator. The truth is, from the beginning God made it so that a man is to copulate with a woman (opposite gender); not the same gender of man in man or women with a woman.

Thus, the result of creature worshiping creature is that God gave them over to "degrading emotions," of impure sexuality of women with women and men in men.

Romans 1:24-27, NASB: ²⁴*Therefore God gave them over in the lusts of their hearts to impurity, **so that their bodies would be dishonored among them**.* ²⁵**For** *they exchanged the truth of God for a lie and **worshiped and served the creature rather than the Creator,** who is blessed forever. Amen.*²⁶**For this reason** *God gave them over to degrading passions; **for their women exchanged the natural function for that which is unnatural,*** ²⁷*and in the same way also the men abandoned the natural function of the woman and burned in their desire toward one another, **men with (lit., in) men** committing **indecent** acts and receiving in their persons the due penalty of their error.*

It is clear that the humans worshipping humans, humans also worshipping animals, human also worshipping trees, humans also worshipping the sun and the moon, and stars, human also worshipping idols and also worshipping demons is creation worshipping creation. God's original intention of worship was opposite creation worship. God's intent is for his creation to worship Him (the only Creator). In addition, Romans 1:27 also calls same-sexuality "indecent." "Indecent" is a compound word that means "disfigured-togetherness.," "deformed-togetherness," or "shameful-togetherness."[45] This is important to know because the beast will also actively recruit for his army from among those who are "indecent."[46]

This Greek word for "indecent" is used only two (2) places in the Bible, and it is only used about the shameful-togetherness of homosexuality and lesbianism. That is, in Revelation 16:15, Jesus inserted a declaration in the middle of the beast's recruiting effort, making it clear that during the season that the dragon, the beast and the false prophet ("another beast") recruits for their army, their focus will be on people whose **shameful-togetherness** is not covered.

Revelation 16:13-16: [13]*And I saw three unclean spirits like frogs [come] out of the mouth of the **dragon**, and out of the mouth of the **beast**, and out of the mouth of the **false prophet**.* [14]*For **they are the spirits of devils, working miracles**, [which] go forth unto the kings of the earth and the whole world, **to gather them to the battle** of that great day of God Almighty.*[15]*Behold, I come as a thief. Blessed [is] he that watches, and keeps his garments, lest he walks naked, and they see his '**shameful-togetherness.**' *[16]*And he gathered them together into a place called in the Hebrew tongue Armageddon.*

Yes, the dragon, the beast, and the false prophet will be

sending out unclean spirits to recruit people for its army; and Jesus declared that they will be looking for people who are not clothed; they will be looking for those exposed with shameful-togetherness!

False Prophets and the Beast

It is clear from Revelation 13 that the false prophet uses false signs to cause people to accepts all the offerings of the beast and its marketing system. The false prophet[47] is also known as "another beast."[48] The false prophet is also called the "antichrist," or the "spirit of antichrist."[49] False prophets also preach the "world", and they preach acceptance of the beast.[50] Also, it is the false prophet who enforces the marketing requirements of the beast.

No one will be able to buy or sell except they have the name of the beast (blasphemy against the God of heaven), or the number of his name (666, the number of blasphemy), or the mark of the beast (the mark of blasphemy).[51] Thus, according to Revelation 13:17-18, merchandising is directly linked to the false prophet, alias, "another beast."

Sad to say, some operate in the Church who have the number of the beast, or the name of the beast, or the mark of the beast in them. In other words, here are some in the Church whose sole purpose is to make the Church of Jesus a marketplace.

Here is the proof. Revelation 13:17-19 indicates that *"no man might buy or sell save he that had the mark, or the name of the beast, or the number of his name."* So, we see that merchandising ("buying and selling") is linked to the beast. 2 Peter 2:1-3 states that *"there were false prophets also among the people, even as there shall be false teachers among you …. ³And through covetousness shall they with 'plastic' words make* **merchandise** *of you ….*

In Revelation 13:11-18 coupled with Revelation 19:20 and Revelation 16:13-14, it was the false prophet, "another beast" that forced people to take on the beast's characteristic to **"buy and sell."**

In 2 Peter 2:1-3, referenced above, that false prophets are the ones **"merchandising"** God's people. Is there a link between these false prophets and the beast? Yes! Any preacher who merchandises the Church of Jesus Christ probably has the name of the beast, the mark of the beast and the number of the beast (666) in their minds and on their hands. Jesus forbids merchandising in the temple, and He cleansed the temple of merchandising at the beginning of His ministry and the end of His ministry.

John 2:13-16: And the Jews' Passover was at hand, and Jesus went up to Jerusalem and found in the temple those that sold oxen and sheep and doves, and the changers of money sitting: And when he had made a scourge of small cords, he drove them all out of the temple, and the sheep, and the oxen; and poured out the changers' money and overthrew the tables; And said unto them that sold doves, Take these things hence; make not my Father's house a house of merchandise.

Matthew 21:10-13: And when he came into Jerusalem, all the city was moved, saying, Who is this? And the multitude said this is Jesus the prophet of Nazareth of Galilee. And Jesus went into the temple of God and **cast out all them that sold and bought** *in the temple, and overthrew the tables of the* *moneychangers, and the seats of them that sold **doves,** And said unto them, It is written, My house shall be called the house of prayer; but ye have made it a den of thieves.*

The number of the beast is linked to the motives as to why people buy and sell. In other words, merchandising in the temple was taking place at the most opportune time for the sellers.

In the days of Jesus, the common people needed to buy animals for their yearly sacrifices. Thus, the sellers in the temple raised their prices during this time; because people were desperate to buy the sacrifices (doves, sheep, ox, etc.) to be used for the atonement of their sins.

It is believed that "Annas" one of the high priests that orchestrated the crucifixion of Jesus was the one merchandising the desperate people. Here is a quote from the *International Standard Bible Encyclopedia, 1915.*

> [Annas] belonged to the Sadducean aristocracy, and, like others of that class, he seems to have been arrogant, astute, ambitious, and enormously wealthy. He and his family were proverbial for their rapacity and greed. The chief source of their wealth seems to have been the sale of requisites for the temple sacrifices, such as sheep, doves, wine, and oil, which they carried on in the four famous "booths of the sons of Annas" on the Mount of Olives, with a branch within the precincts of the temple itself. During the great feasts, they were

34

able to extort high monopoly prices for theft goods. Hence, our Lord's strong denunciation of those who made the house of prayer "a den of robbers" (Mark 11:15-19), and the curse in the Talmud, "Woe to the family of Annas! Woe to the serpent-like hisses" (Pes 57a)."

Those who have the number of the beast do the same today. They are mercilessly selling (merchandising) things of the Spirit ("doves") to desperate saints. This is seen during the time of conferences; books, CDs, memorabilia, and so on are all for sale at disproportionate prices.

If Jesus was here in the flesh, he would drive out the merchandisers from their booths and buildings. Am I saying that men of God should not sell their material at all? No! The book of Proverb said to buy wisdom.

What. I am saying is that it does not appear that we should merchandise the Church at inappropriate times. Preachers should not treat the Church as an emporium, only for buying a selling. Today, people even sell prophecies in the Church; there is the $25 line, the $500 line, the $1000, line, etcetera.

The Righteousness of Jesus

Jesus' righteous-acts gives us the victory out-of-the beast and its system. In other words, as we declare Jesus' righteousness, some will believe into Jesus and come out of the beast and its system. In Revelation 15, those who had gotten the victory out of the beast, song the song of the Lamb of God. In this song, they revealed what will cause the nations to worship God. They declared, *"for all nations will come and worship before You, for Your **righteous acts have been revealed."***

That is, it appears that the reason they were delivered out of the beast; and to stand on the sea of glass mixed with fire, worshipping God was/is because of the righteous acts of the Lamb of God. One of these righteous acts of Jesus is His righteousness imparted to the believer through faith in Jesus Christ, and faith in the blood of Jesus that was shed for us.

Romans 3:21-22:[21]*But now the **righteousness**[5] **of God** without the law **is manifested,** being witnessed by the law and the prophets;* [22]*Even the righteousness of God by the faith of Jesus Christ unto all and upon all them that believe for there is no difference.*

---

[5] Lit., "dikaiosune," a compound word of dikaios + sun — righteous-togetherness

Revelation 15:2-4, NASB: *²And I saw something like a sea of glass mixed with fire, and those who had been victorious **over** the beast and his image and the number of his name, standing on the sea of glass, holding harps of God. ³And they sang the song of Moses, the bond-servant of God, and **the song of the Lamb**, saying, …. ⁴" Who will not fear, O Lord, and glorify Your name? For You alone are holy; For ALL THE NATIONS WILL COME AND WORSHIP BEFORE YOU, **FOR YOUR RIGHTEOUS ACTS HAVE BEEN REVEALED."***

We see in the reference above that some were victorious over (lit., out-of) the beast and some things associated with the beast. Then the victors proceeded to sing the song of Moses and the song of the Lamb. The song of Moses is found in Exodus 15, which was sung after God defeated Pharaoh and his "600" chosen chariots in the Red Sea. This principle will be developed in another chapter.

However, it appears to me that "the song of the Lamb" is the song in Revelation 15:3-4, references the "righteous-acts" of God. One of God's righteous-acts is explained in Romans 3:21-22. In short, God imparted to us "His righteousness" through Jesus; because Jesus has made us "righteous" as long as we are "together" with Jesus and remain in Jesus, through faith. Again, it is a "righteousness-togetherness" that is only received by faith in Jesus, because of the righteous-acts of Jesus. More importantly, in Romans 3:22, Paul makes it clear that there is no "distinction" with God when it comes to those who accept Christ's righteous-act of His righteousness-togetherness gifted to us through faith. God saves anyone "who believes that Jesus is the Christ,"[52] even those who were once given over to the beast, but now believe. In the freedom "out-of" the beast, through the righteousness of the Lamb of God, who takes away the sin of the world;[53] those who were victorious out of the beast, worship God and the Lamb with their harps, singing of the righteous-acts of Jesus. The gave God credit because He caused them to be victorious out of the beast and its system.

With that said, the righteousness of Jesus Christ imparted to us, the "righteous-acts," or the "acts-of His righteousness," also has other meanings. That is, according to Romans 1:30, a righteous-act (singular) of God also implies the potential of judgment by death for those who continue in the beast system (worshipping of idols and images rather than the Living God) by not repenting of their works. That is, sometimes the fear of death, may cause some to repent of beastly deeds.

The book of Jude[54] implies that we can save some with mercy, and we may save some with fear. Thus, Jesus' righteous acts have two veins of operations. One is through the potential of punishment of death for those who continue in the beast and its system. The other is that Jesus also offers the grace-gift of justification[55] through His righteous-act of giving us life instead of the death of Adam.

This is seen in Romans, chapter 5; and is summarized in Romans 5:18. Yes, one of the righteous acts of Jesus is the

38

gift of justification He gives us, through His sacrifice on the cross unto eternal life through faith in Jesus Christ.

Thus, the righteous acts of God can be felt either in a negative way — he judges those who reject His existence, and they worship idols/images instead. The other side of the righteous acts of God is that he will give life to those who accept the sacrifice of Jesus, who was crucified for us. It follows that those on the sea of glass mixed with fire who were victorious out-of-the beast may have experienced the righteous-acts of God in both ways. This is also clearly seen in the two approaches the Lord of the harvest employed in Revelation 14, and His harvest resulted in the victory out-of-the beast for those standing on the sea of glass mixed with fire.

The Sea of Glass for Priests

In Revelation 15:2, those who were victorious out of the beast through the righteousness of Jesus Christ, by faith in Jesus also had to be washed. This is true for **all** believers.

Once we believe, we must be baptized in water, baptized in the Holy Spirit and fire. They were being washed in/upon the sea of glass mixed with fire. The washing in the sea has many applications related to baptisms and washings.

1. They were being washed in the baptism of the Holy Spirit and fire.[56]
2. They were being washed/baptized spiritually, as "priests" in the Molten Sea.[57]
3. They were being washed, replicating the principle of baptism in the Red Sea (lit.; the Termination Sea),[58]
4. They were being washed in the apostolic ("sent") pool[59] — The Molten Sea was mounted on the back of twelve Ox,[60] representing the support of apostolic ministries that restores sight through the washing of the water of the revelation of Jesus Christ.

With that said, my focus in this section will be on the Molten Sea and the Red Sea, and that very briefly. Solomon built a "Molten Sea"[61] for the temple. The Hebrew word for "molten" is also translated as "hard"[62] in the book of Job. Thus, as the sea in Revelation was made of glass, and therefore "solid" or hard" surface area. The sea of glass is symbolized in the Molten-hard Sea.

The sea of glass was also mixed with "fire," which also corresponds to Solomon **"molten (liquefied by heat) sea."** Also, "the sea" that Solomon made was used for washing. However, it was used for washing "priests."[63] This is a significant point.

The overcomers in Revelation 15:2 were now considered "priest"[64] of God; and thus, had to be washed in the fire, or baptized in the fire in preparation to serve the living God in the things of God. The sea of glass mixed with fire also pertains to the Red Sea. This can be confirmed by the fact that they also sang the song of Moses in Revelation 15:2-4. Moses sang his song after God defeated the Egyptian in the Red Sea as depicted in Exodus 14 and Exodus 15.

1 Corinthians 10:2, said that the Israelites were "baptized into Moses" when they walk on dry ground through the Red Sea. Thus, the overcomers in Revelation 15:2, were also baptized into God and the Lamb of God on the sea of glass mixed with fire. And, as important as the baptism in fire, the effect of the baptism of fire on the sea of glass must also be understood.

That is, in the days of Moses, Pharaoh and his 600 [part of the number of the beast **600-60-6 (666)**] chariots were destroyed in the Red Sea; and the enemies of Israel were never seen again, because God destroyed them in the sea. The same is true for the overcomers in Revelation 15:2, and all who are baptized into Jesus Christ, once they overcame the beast, and once they were baptized, God destroyed/burned their past beastly life in the sea mixed with fire. Their past relative to the beast could no longer chase them, as the Egyptians could no longer chase Moses and the Israelites!

Their past life with the beast, as beasts, was 'terminated,' and burned up. They now had a new life, an exchanged life with Christ! The same is true for any believer, once you are baptized into Jesus, your past and any guilty thoughts chasing you from the past is "terminated," through the baptism of fire into Jesus. To solidify this truth further, the Hebrew word for the word "Red[65]" (in the Red Sea) is translated as the "'Termination' Sea" or the "'End' Sea." What or who did God "end" or "terminate" in the sea? God ended the enemy's pursuit of the Israelites. God ended the life of Pharaoh and Pharaoh's 600[66] select chariots in the sea. This is, God ended the chase of the number of the beast (represented in the number 600). The Israelites saw their persecutors and enslavers no more; because the termination sea destroyed them! Saying, it as it is written in the epistle to the Colossians, believers are *"buried with [Jesus] in baptism, in which you were also raised with Him through faith …. He **disarmed** the rulers and* authorities ..." (Colossians 2:12-15). Here is Peter's take on baptism. *"Corresponding to that, **baptism now saves you** – not the removal of dirt from the flesh, **but an appeal to God for a good conscience** – through the resurrection of Jesus Christ"* (1 Peter 3:21).

It follows that God freed the overcomer in Revelation 15:2 out of the beast; and He freed them from their past actions. Their past will no longer be haunting them; because of the righteousness of Jesus that was imparted to them through faith in Jesus, and through the baptism of fire into Jesus Christ. The sea mixed with fire will burn up any residue of sin.

*Hebrews 10:17: And their sins and lawless deeds I will remember **no** more.*

The Harvest

In Revelation 14:9-13, we read that a "third angel" was sent to declare a specific message concerning beast worship and the mark of the beast. The warning from the angel is not to worship the beast, the beast's image, and not to receive the beast's mark.

The angel also indicated that there would be some consequences if a person chose to worship the beast, its image and chose to take its mark. Here are the consequences:

1. The person would drink the "un-governed" wrath of God (lit., sacrifice-anger of God).
2. Torment with brimstone (lit., torment with divine-lightning or torment with divine-fire, or torment with divine Sulphur smell)
3. The smoke of their torment would go up forever
4. They will not have the ability to have "rest" (pause) in their lives.

Also, the angel encourages the saints to persevere in the face of death and to keep the faith of-Jesus (the same faith Jesus demonstrated in the face of death). That is, it was very clear from Revelation 13:15 that the penalty was death, for all who do not worship the beast, its image or take its mark. Hence, the voice from heaven, in Revelation 14:13, encouraging the saints who resist the beast saying, "Blessed are the dead **which die in the Lord from now on**! Yes, says the Spirit, so that they may rest

44

from their labors and their work do follow them." With that said, it was immediately after the third angel made his evangelistic declaration, and the voice came from heaven, we read of the two (2) harvest taking place. In Revelation 14:14-16, we read that one harvest was administered by "one like the son of man;" and in Revelation 14:17-20, another harvest as administered by an angel.

It appears to me that the "one like the son of man" represents Jesus and the methods (sickle) Jesus used to win souls. These methods can be seen in all four of the Gospels (Matthew, mark, Luke, and John).

Jesus' Harvest Sickle (just to name a few)

Love	Truth	Faith	Light
Compassion	Glory	Mercy	Forgiveness
Miracles	Signs	Wonders	Crucifixion
Resurrection	Life	Sonship	Holy Spirit

The "one like the son of man" may also represent those in the Church, who mature[67] to become "like" Jesus; and who also evangelize (harvest) using the same method Jesus used in the four Gospels.

However, the second harvest administered by the angel, in Revelation 14:17-20, may not have been by the same method (sickle) as the one like the son of man. It appears that according to Revelation 14:20, severity was applied in this reaping of the vine of the earth during the second harvest. In fact, if one would search out in the Scriptures, "horse bridle" that were used on some of those who were reaped from the earth (specifically James 3:3), one would see that one of the purposes of the severity in Revelation 14:20 is to produce "faith" and "persuasion" unto obedience.

Thus, as one continues to read from Revelation 14:9 through Revelation 15:4, it becomes apparent that the people on the sea of glass mixed with fire were apparently people who were harvested by "one like the son of man" with his sharp sickle, and also people harvested by the other angel, with his sharp sickle. It appears that there were two (2) different wisdom principles of evangelism used of His "variegated wisdom;" and yes, they yielded victorious results unto the Lord of the harvest, Jesus, the Christ!

*Revelation 14:16: Then He [one like the son of man] who sat on the cloud swung His sickle over the earth, and **the earth was reaped.***

*Revelation 14:20: So, the angel swung his sickle to the earth and **gathered [the clusters from] the vine of the earth and** threw them into the great winepress of the wrath of God.*

*Revelation 15:2 And I saw something like a sea of glass mixed with fire, and those who had been victorious **'out-of'** the beast and his image and the number of his name, standing on the sea of glass, holding harps of God.*

46

Afterword, the Eight King

This "afterword" is intended to provide more detail ("meat," maybe, for some) with regards to the beast and its present application, and future application relative to "world-governments."[68]

*Revelation 17:3, NIV: Then the angel carried me away in the Spirit into a desert. There I saw a woman sitting on a scarlet beast that was covered with **blasphemous names** and had **seven heads** and ten horns.*

The beast that John saw in the reference above consisted of seven heads. The seven heads represent seven kings.[69] The eighth king was "**out-of**" one of the seven kings that previously existed. That is, the leopard beast, which is also called a scarlet beast, existed before, it also died, and it will somehow be resurrected again. So, a question must be asked: is the resurrection of the beast-king spiritual or literal, God knows? With that said, let us review the Scriptures.

When John, the beloved, saw the vision, he became "astonished" at the woman who carried the beast and the beast.[70] The angel then said, *"Why are you astonished? I will **explain** to you the **mystery** of the **woman** and the **beast** she rides, which has the seven heads and ten horns"* (Revelation 17:7). Thus, the angel began his explanation with an interesting remark. He gave his explanation by saying the "mystery ... beast" **once** existed.

Revelation 17:8a, **NIV:** *The beast, which you saw,* ***once was,*** *now is not, and* ***will*** *come up* ***out of*** *the* ***Abyss*** *and go to his destruction.*

The Scripture is clear. The beast **"once was."** This means he once lived, yet **"now is not."** He died from a stroke of death, as seen in Revelation 13.:14 Finally, he **"will come up out of the Abyss."** This appears to be the beast's resurrection or resurgence. The Holy Writ plainly says that the beast will come out of the Abyss. It also says that the eighth beast **"once was."** That is, this beast lived before.

Revelation 17:9-10, **NIV:** *⁹This calls for the mind of wisdom. The seven* ***heads are*** *seven hills* ***(lit., mountains)*** *on which the woman sits.* *¹⁰They are also* ***seven kings. Five*** *have fallen,* ***one*** *is, the* ***other*** *has not yet come; but when he does come, he must remain for a little while.*

The seven heads of the beast are seven, "mountains;" the heads are also representative of seven **kings.** At the time when John saw the vision, **five** of these kings had "fallen." The **sixth** king existed when John saw the vision. This tells us that the beast with its six heads (kings) including his blasphemous name existed in John's time[6].

---

[6] This is important to know that John was not affected by the mark of the beast, neither the beast name or number, even though the sixth head of beast existed in John's days. The Roman Empire ruled most of the habitable world of that time and hence, the sixth head relates to a king of the Roman rule — the fourth beast. This sixth king is believed to be Emperor Nero.

The beast with its seventh head, however, did not exist at the time John saw the vision. Now note: As previously indicated in this manuscript, Daniel, said there will be a total of four (4) beasts throughout man's apparent rule in the earth until the fifth (5th) kingdom (the kingdom of God, the Stone Kingdom) completely replace the beasts' rule. The four beasts, identified by Daniel, covers all the ages up until "the kingdoms of this world become our Lord's and his Christ's."[71] Beasts' rule also appears to exist until the Lamb of God arrests and remove the "eighth beast," sending it/him to the lake of fire. Thus, in every age, there is a beast with its head (a king and/or a political leader) that rules. Thus, I believe that the beast with its "**seventh**[72] **head**" rules after the sixth king-beast until the eighth beast rises. However, the eighth beast is a little different.

*Revelation 17:11, NIV: The beast who once was [he lived] and now is not [he died], is an eighth king. He **belongs** to the seven and is going to destruction.*

The word translated "**belongs**" is a compound of two Greek words. The two Greek words are "**eimi**" which means, "**to exist**" and "**ek**" which means "**out of.**" The phrase reads, "He **exists out of** the seven." This means that even though he is the eighth king, he lived (existed) once already in the form of one of the seven kings. Therefore, he is "'**out-of'** the seven." In Chapter 13:1, John saw the beast come out of the sea of humanity. John saw him as a leopard with feet like a bear and a mouth like a lion. John did not stop there with his description. John continued saying: *"One of the heads of the beast seemed to have had a **fatal wound**, but the fatal wound had been **healed**. The whole world was astonished and followed the beast"* (Revelation 13:3, NIV).

Two things I will interpret from this verse. "**One** of the **heads** seems to have a **fatal wound**." The King James Version says, *"And I saw one of his heads as it were **wounded to death**."* This is key for understanding this verse. "**Fatal wound**" or "wounded to death" in the Greek reads "**stroke of death**." "**Death**" in this verse is in the **genitive case (source), or possessive case.** This tells us that death is the **source (genitive case)** of the wound. This phrase may also read: the beast.... had a **stroke from death or death's stroke.** In other words, the angel or spirit of Death is the one who struck the beast; or this wound was caused by Death. Saying it another, Death is the source of the wound.

The Scripture also says this "fatal wound had been **healed.**" His wound was indeed healed; yet there is more to his healing. "Healed" is the Greek word transliterated in English as "**therapeutics," or "therapy.**" A person who receives **therapy** is being served (attended) by a therapist. The therapist is trying to preserve — heal — the person by attending to the injured or wounded; sometimes by exercising, movements, and so on.

So, it appears that the stroke from Death was **therapeutic** for the beast. The literal rendition tells us that the death-stroke "served as an attendant" for the beast. In other words, the sword was used to kill the beast to **preserve** the beast for future use; and/or, it was preserved to be potentially resurrected. The Scripture says that those deceived by "another beast" made an image of the beast that died, yet he lived. How was this beast able to "yet live" again; except it previously died?

Revelation 13:14, NIV: Because of the signs he ["another beast"] was given the power to do on behalf of the first beast, he deceived the inhabitants of the earth. He ordered them to set up an image in honor of the beast who 'has the plague of' the sword and yet lived.

The image the people made was not for all seven heads of the beast. The image was only for the beast that was wounded by the sword and **yet lived.** The fact that the beast "yet lived," even though he died, helped to convince some inhabitants earth to make an image to the beast. Why? The beast's resurrection ("ascension" out of the Abyss) deceived them; that is, it died, yet it lived again, in addition to the death threat and pseudo signs of the false prophet, alias, "another beast."

*Revelation 17:8, NIV: The beast, which you saw, once was, now is not, and will **come up out of the Abyss** and go to his destruction. The inhabitants of the earth whose names have not been written in the book of life from the creation of the world will be **astonished** when they see the beast because he **once was,** now is not, **and yet will come.***

One of the ways the beast will rise from the abyss appears to be in someone's body. It appears that the beast (personified) will possess a "body." Or, should I say, there will be a body prepared for this beast. Allow me to give you an example concerning Cain. Eve thought that she had gotten a man (Cain) from the Lord when she birthed Cain.

*Genesis 4:1, NIV: Adam lay with his wife Eve, and she became pregnant and gave birth to Cain. She said, "With the **help** of the Lord I have brought forth a man."*

This was a tragic birth. Eve did not realize that Cain was the seed of the wicked one.[73] She thought God "helped" her to bring him forth. The Church of Jesus later learned that Cain belonged to the evil one (Satan).

*1 John 3:12, NIV: Do not be like **Cain, who belonged to the evil one** and murdered his brother.*

The word "belonged" is the Greek word "ek," which means "out of" with the idea of the object having its origin from within the entity it is out of. Therefore, Cain was "'out-of' the evil one.". Tragically, there are human bodies that are born on the earth who are Satan's children.

God said to the serpent that He (God) would put enmity between the serpent's offspring and Eve's.[74] The serpent does indeed have offspring.[75] Jesus calls them the "children of the wicked one."[76] Jesus also called Judas a "Devil."[77] Judas' body was possessed by Satan more than once, during Judas' betrayal of Jesus.[78] With that said, it does appear that the spirit of a beast that died can be resurrected into a body prepared for him. This should not

52

be strange. Remember, the second beast, alias, false prophet, also gave "spirit" to a dumb idol, and the image spoke.[79] This will be a significant false sign.[80] That is, there will come a time when the activity of Satan will intensify with false signs, false wonders, false power, that will function through the mystery of lawlessness.[81]

The book of Daniel, Chapter 8:1-21, also exemplified the truth reviewed above. That is, Daniel saw in a vision a beast that represents Greece and a spirit that was behind Greece. Daniel saw a vision of **Greece** attacking Media and Persia, in the form of a "hairy male-goat" attacking a ram. The male-goat (which is an allegory that includes the natural King of Greece and the invisible prince of Greece[82]) originally had one horn. This horn was the **first** king. *"And the **rough goat is the king of Grecia:** and the **great horn** that is between his eyes is the **first king"** (Daniel 8:21, KJV). After the horn (Alexander, the great) was broken (he died), four (4) came up after him, and eventually another little horn. It is this event that I will use to demonstrate the death and resurrection of the beast.

*Daniel 8:8, NIV: The **goat** became very great, but at the height of his power his large horn was **broken** off, and in its place, four prominent horns grew up toward the four **winds of heaven.***

The **goat** that became "very **great**" is Alexander, **the great,** of Greece.[83] Alexander died at a young age, around 33 years old, represented by the "horn that was broken." This happened at the peak of Alexander's power. **So, the goat and the great horn represents Alexander, the great, with the understanding that the horn was broken, but the goat did do die**. After Alexander's death, four (4) other rulers (his generals) took the helm of the Grecian kingdom. They eventually separated the kingdom of Alexander into four divisions.

This is what is meant by the phrase "towards the four winds of heaven." In Daniel 7, they are represented by the "four heads" of the leopard beast. It was out of this setting that Daniel began to describe some last day events.

*Daniel 8:9, KJV: And out of **one** of them came forth **a little** horn, which waxed exceeding great, towards the south, and toward the east, and the pleasant land.*

The word **"one"** in Daniel 8:9 means **"united."** As an ordinal, the same word is also used as **"first"** in the Hebrew language, according to Strong's Concordance (see OT #259). The word **"one"** is the same word translated as **"a"**, referenced above. The word **"little"** means "littleness," "petty (in size or number)," **"adv. a short (time)"** [Strong's #4704; #4705].

The Hebrew definitions above are significant, concerning Revelation 17:8, which says, the beast **"once was,** now is not and **will** come out of the Abyss." It is also important to know that the beast will only be in power for **"one hour."**[84] By inserting the Strong's definitions in Daniel 8:9

the verse would read, *"And out of 'united' of [the four horns] came forth the **"first"** (king) as a little horn for a 'short time.'* **"Short time"** may equate to the "one hour" in Revelation 17:12.

Revelation says the beast "once was;" this appears to be the **"first king"** mentioned in Daniel 8:21, who existed **before** in the form of Alexander, the Great. Revelation 17 also says the beast that "once was" will "walk up out of the Abyss;" and that he was **"out-of"** the previous seven kings. This again points to the **"first** king" in Daniel who will arise again in the form of **"another** horn."

The word "another" as an **"ordinal"** by definition means **"first."** Thus, **the horn** of Daniel 8:9, which is called "another" may be understood to be the ruling spirit of the "first" king, Alexander.

The **spirit** of Greece[85] will arise again for a **"short"** time or for "one **hour"** in another **body, or another form of the leopard beast-kingdom.** Hopefully, you understand this. If not, let me review again. Alexander had died suddenly. His kingdom was **divided** under four generals. The four divided kingdoms may potentially be **united** again to cover the lands of the ancient conquests, for so the word "one," in Daniel 8:9, is also defined.

"Out of **united** of them came **first** horn." Out of the **united** Greco dominion, which shall start "**little"** at first, the demon-goat (spirit of Greece) that controlled the **"first"** king shall manifest again in the form of **"another** horn." According to Revelation 13, it shall dominate and make war in the earth for forty-two months.

I have heard doctrines which indicate that the so-called antichrist[86] the beast will come out of Syria. The Scripture teaches differently, and it is the Scriptures that I will use to show the truth. First, once must understand that the antichrist is different from the leopard beast. The antichrist is indeed a beast; however, he is "another beast," (a spirit, the false prophet, or the beast, the false prophet) not the "first (leopard) beast."

With that said, in Daniel 8, he saw the king of Greece as a "goat" which he later called a "**rough** goat" or a "shaggy goat" which is also literally translated "**demon-goat**" or "**devil goat.**" (I will come back to this later.) In Daniel's discourse, he said the "large" or "great horn" was broken. Daniel did not say that the goat died, or the goat was broken. If the goat had died, the other four horns could not have grown in the goat. Even nature teaches that for goat's horns to grow, the goat has to be living.

The Goat kingdom lived on after Alexander died. This means that the same "prince of Greece" that ruled Alexander, also ruled in and over the four division of Alexander's kingdom. The Hebrew says the four horns (the four generals) grew up "**under him**" (the goat). Thus, the spirit of Greece will also again be manifested in the "little horn." In Daniel 8:21 the angel said, *"The shaggy goat is the king of Greece."* Yet, in the same breath, the angel said, *"the **large horn** between his eyes **is the first*** *king."* The shaggy goat is the king of Greece, and the large horn between his eyes is the first king. Is there a difference between the "king of Greece" and the "first King?"

If there is a distinction, the goat, "king of Greece, must represent an invisible spirit principality;[87] and, the first king (the great horn) represents Alexander, the great. Remember, there is a spirit behind every beast king or beast kingdom. There is "king Heylel" — the king of (mystery) Babylon (Isaiah 14:4-12). There is an invisible "'chief' of Persia" or the invisible "kings of Persia" (Daniel 10:13). There is the invisible "prince of Greece" (Daniel 10:20). There is the **"spirit** of the **kings** of the Medes."** (Jeremiah 51:11).

Yet, it appears that the goat and the large horn represent the first king of Greece. This means even though the horn was broken, meaning, the first king died; yet the character of the first king or the spirit of Greece lived in the form of the **shaggy goat.** Do you see this? This may seem contradictory, but it is not. The visions of God convey variegated wisdom. So, it was the large horn that was broken, not the **shaggy** goat.

Thus, out of the king who had died (yet he is still living in the form of the shaggy goat) came forth the four other horns; and eventually the final little horn. The leopard beast of Revelation has similar characteristics. That is, even though seven kings or "heads" of the beast died, the beast still lives on (even in this age); and eventually, one of the previous heads that died will ascend **'out-of'** the abyss — the place of death.[88]

As stated above, the four horns came up "under him," out of the same source — the apparent demon-goat. Then, eventually, out of these "united" horns will come forth the **first** horn **again.** This can be understood because the spirit of Alexander or the spirit of Greece was preserved in the form of the shaggy goat. Remember, the goat **is** also representative of the king of Greece.

It will be out of the "king of Greece" (the "shaggy goat") that "another" horn, or should I say, the "first" horn, will arise. Remember, "another" as an ordinal means "first." Therefore, the leopard beast will arise again or resurge into dominion out of the king of Greece or the spirit of Greece. That is, **"the way is being made for the spirit of Greece"** to have dominion again. With that's said, let us now review the shaggy goat as it may also symbolize a demon spirit.

The word "shaggy" or "rough" is the Hebrew word transliterated **satyr.** A **satyr** among **Greek** mythology is supposed to be a horse's or goat's body with a human upper body and head. This word is translated "demons' in the **margin** of the New International Version; and as "devils" in the King James Version; and goat-demons in the New Revised Standard Version, in Leviticus 17:7.

*Leviticus 17:7, KJV: And they shall no more offer their sacrifices unto **devils**, after whom they have gone-a-whoring. This shall be a statute forever unto them throughout their generations.*

*Leviticus 17:7, NIV: ⁷They must no longer offer any of their sacrifices to the goat **idols**⁷ to whom they prostitute themselves. This is to be a lasting ordinance for them and for the generations to come.*

*Leviticus 17:7, NASB: "They shall no longer sacrifice their sacrifices to **the goat demons** with which they play the harlot. This shall be a permanent statute to them throughout their generations."'*

Therefore, the "rough" or "shaggy" goat is also symbolic of a **demon-**goat. This demon-goat is a king because he is called the king of Greece. There is an invisible "prince of Greece."[89] He is the principality over Greece. It appears that this spirit will come to power again in the similitude of Alexander, the Great.

It will go from a small entity to influencing the gathering the "kings of the whole world" with its "frog-like" **spirit.**[90] The beast will be manifested mixed with a demon, or the beast may also mutate into different spirit forms — the spirit prince of Greece,[91] or a demon-goat,[92] or a leopard beast,[93] a scarlet-colored beast,[94] a frog demon.[95] Remember, the "shaggy" or "rough goat" was not annihilated. It was preserved in the abyss or sea of

---

⁷ NIV margin for "idols" is "demons"

humanity for the appointed time, as we learn in Revelation 13 and Revelation 17. Thus, the leopard beast that will rise will not walk in its power; because another power will be with the beast.

Daniel 8:22-24, NIV: *[22]The four horns that replaced the one that was broken off represent four kingdoms that will emerge from his nation but will not have the same power. [23]"In the latter part of their reign, when rebels have become completely wicked, a stern-faced king, a master of intrigue, will arise. [24]**He will become very strong, but not by his own power.** He will cause astounding devastation and will succeed in whatever he does. He will destroy the mighty men and holy people."*

The kingdom of Greece that was divided into four rulers did not have the same power as Alexander. This power was reserved for another king — the beast. The beast from the Abyss will become strong, **"but not by his own power."** Whose "power" is it then? It will be by the power of the goat-demon. It will be the power of Satan.[96] It will be the same spirit that empowered Alexander. Ironically, one of the symbols of satanic worship is a goat.

*Revelation 13:2: "And the beast which I saw was like unto a leopard, and his feet were as the feet of a bear, and his mouth as the mouth of a lion: and **the dragon** gave him his **power,** and his seat, and **great authority.**"*

Thus, you can see that Satan is involved in the rule of the leopard beast. Satan gave the beast his power and authority, and the beast will destructively use that power and authority. Here are some of the diverse characteristics of the leopard beast. The beast, a "leopard," (deathly stealth by apparent transparency); it has the "feet of a bear" (slow-moving with the ability to rip and grip) and "mouth of a lion" (mouth of blasphemy). Keep in mind that the book of Daniel described the Greek empire in different forms. First Nebuchadnezzar saw Greece is his vision as **"one of bronze"** (Daniel 2:39). Daniel saw this same kingdom as **"a leopard"** (Daniel 7:6). Finally, the kingdom of Greece is also seen as a **"goat"** (Daniel 8:5).

In Revelation, the beast is called a leopard, bear, and lion, which are the characteristic of **three** beasts of Daniel 7 that will be in the "eighth" beast. The beast (the spirit of Greece, or the spirit of Greece in a man, or the governmental philosophy of Greece) will be manifested in diverse forms.

With all that said, I will now give some understanding of Alexander, the great, as he relates to the beast and mystery Babylon. I will begin with some historical facts. Alexander is the **first great** king of the Greeks, even though; his father Philip was the first to unite Greece. Alexander's name means **"defender of man" or "man-defender."** The number of the beast is the number **'because of' man (666).** Alexander is also known as a **man of war**, as the beast will be an apparent war machine.

He was one of the last kings who led the battles in front of the armies. Once Alexander conquered most of the known world, he made **Babylon** his capital. He suddenly

died at the peak of his rule. These statements are historical facts. The beauty of this knowledge is: God prophesied it in the Bible (Daniel 10 and Daniel 11). These historical facts of Alexander can also aid in understanding the book of Revelation and the book Daniel. I will begin with **Babylon.**

When the angel showed John the vision of the prostitute, the angel called her "Mystery **Babylon**" (Revelation 17:5). The beast was carrying Babylon in the form of a woman (Revelation 17:7). She is sitting on the seven heads of the beast that the angel calls "mountains." "The seven heads **are seven mountains** on which the woman sits" (Revelation 17:9). Some say the woman represents the Vatican that sits on seven hills. The Vatican does sit on seven hills; however, there is a broader perspective with regards to "mountains."

A continent is the top of a mountain. The ocean covers the mountain bottom. This is why the further a person goes from the beach, the deeper the water becomes, the broader the base. For example, islands are the top of mountains. The mountains "broader" bases are covered by the Sea. This is true for all continents. The continent we live on, here in the Americas, is the narrower head of a mountain, even as large as this continent is. The broader base of the continent of the Americas is beneath the sea. Yes, the water covers the mountain base deep in the ocean. Therefore, the seven mountains could represent the seven continents **or all** the kingdoms that exist on the earth. I say "all" because in the Hebrew language seven is defined as "complete." We will also see shortly that the Scriptures also interpret the mountains as peoples.

The beast, **temporarily**,[97] rules these mountaintops — the continents of nations. "He was given authority over **every** tribe, people, language, and **nation**" (Revelation 13:7). I would say this is the **whole** world or all seven continents. "Mystery Babylon" sat on these seven "mountains" which the bible interprets to be also "many waters," "peoples, multitudes, nations, and languages."

*Revelation 17:1 … I will show you the judgment of the great harlot who **sits on many waters***

*Revelation 17:3: …. and I saw a woman **sitting on a scarlet beast**, full of blasphemous names, **having seven heads** and ten horns.*

*Revelation 17:9: … **The seven heads are seven mountains on which the woman sits.***

*Revelation 7:15: And he said to me, "The **waters** which you saw where the harlot sits, **are peoples and multitudes and nations and tongues**."*

Babylon is also the **religious and commercial** center of the beast, just as **Babylon** became the capital of Alexander. The scripture also says, "The woman you saw is the great city that **rules** over the **kings** of the **world**."[98] The "city" [Babylon] is part of the variegated religious and marketing machine for the beast. The beast will use

Mystery Babylon until the beast eventually turns against the harlot woman.[99] That is, the beast will eventually turn against the religious systems of the world.[100]

Alexander is also known as a **man of war.** He was such a fierce fighter that he won wars that should have been lost, even though we know that God gave him these victories by providence (Daniel 2:21). Nonetheless, when the **world** worshipped the resurrected beast, they feared him because the beast had a **warlike** nature.

Hear the Scripture: *"They also worshipped the beast and asked, 'Who is like the beast? Who can make **war against him?'"** (Revelation 13:4b). Like Alexander, the beast will be a "**furious**" warrior.

Daniel 8:7, NIV: I [Daniel] saw him [Alexander] **attack** *the ram (Mede and Persia)* **furiously** *striking the ram and shattering his two horns. The ram was powerless to stand against him; the goat knocked him to the ground and* **trampled** *on him, and none could rescue from his power.*

The reader should also compare Daniel 7:23-24. The fourth kingdom on the earth will "devour," trample and crush the earth (See Daniel 7:23). The beast will also come on the scene by **subduing** (or to hamstring) three other kings (see Daniel 7:24). The beast from the abyss will be a furious warrior against the "mighty men and **holy people**" (Daniel 8:24).

With that said, another important note is that Alexander also suddenly died. This, I believe, is the "stroke of death" that killed the beast (a king and his kingdom) referenced in Revelation 13. This kingdom will be raised from the dead. Alexander died at an early age — 33. This, I believe, in light of Revelation 13 was to preserve the spirit of his kingdom until the time of the eighth beast. Do not forget, the eighth beast was **"ek"** — **out of** the seven. Vines Expository Dictionary says **"ek"** carries with it the idea of "originating from within."

Thus, the eighth king originated from **within (ek — out of)** one of the seven kings. "The beast who once was…is an eighth king."[101] I believe the eighth beast that once was is the spirit of Greece (principality of Greece according to Daniel 10) that dominated Alexander the Great. The same spirit that dominated Alexander will again influence the "opinion" of the eighth beast and its ten horns.

Allow me to tell you about an event.

I was on an extended fast. There was a lot of warfare; and about the ninth day, I sat weak on the sofa as my wife prepared some chicken soup for me. As I waited for the soup to be prepared, I saw a vision.

In the vision, the voice said, "The way is being made for the **spirit of Greece.**" I also understood that some heart-breaking things would happen in America.[102] The voice then said after the events in America occurred, "I will bring forth the boy scouts."

The point I wanted to bring out is, **"the way is being made for the spirit of Greece."** The beliefs of the early Greeks shall be a way of life.

History teaches us that the ancient Greeks, especially some of the wealthy women, believed that lesbianism or homosexuality[103] were normal. This attitude is widespread today. The main god of the Greeks was homosexual. It was a practice among the Greek for "males" to pursue "beautiful" young boys to have intercourse with them (turning the young boys into catamites). History also tells us that Alexander had a male companion most of his life; even though he eventually got married to a woman before his death. The spirit of Greece and the Greek nation will again be prominent. The Lord made this clear in Daniel 8. We learn that a "stern-faced king" will rise out of Greece.[104]

The Church must guard against the attitude of the prince of Greece. Refer to the Bible or go to the library and study the culture of ancient Greece. You may be surprised how today's world is **governed** by the "wisdom," principles, and spirituality of the Greeks.

In conclusion, the beast will be an advocate, on behalf of rebellious **mankind, against** God. They will eventually make war against the Lamb of God. However, the beast will be unsuccessful in this attempt to fight the Lamb of God because the Lamb of God will overcome the dragon, the beast, the beast's army, and the false prophet.

*Revelation 17:14, NASB: "These will wage war against the Lamb, and **the Lamb will overcome** them, because He is Lord of lords and King of kings, and those who are with Him [are the] called and chosen and faithful."*

Jesus is Lord! Jesus is King! The Lamb of God will overcome all!

Prayer opportunity:

If you are not sure if you will partake of any of the resurrections before the resurrection of eternal judgment, here is a prayer you can pray. "I confess with my mouth that the Lord Jesus is the Christ, and I believe in my heart that Jesus died for my sins and that God has raised Jesus from the dead for my justification. Because, in my heart, I believe that Jesus is the Christ unto righteousness and with my mouth, confession is made unto salvation." Amen! *(See 1 John 5:1 w/Rom 10:9-10)*

Name of the person praying: _____

Date and Time of Prayer: _____

ENDNOTES

[1] Daniel 2

[2] Daniel 4:16, Ecclesiastes 3:18, and contrast Daniel 7:4, in which a man's heat was given to the lion beats which I believe represents Nebuchadnezzar's worship of the God of Israel, the same God of Jesus and Jesus' Church.

[3] Luke 13:31-32

[4] Daniel 7

[5] Daniel 7:1-6; Daniel 7:15; Daniel 7:23

[6] Daniel 2 and Daniel 7 indicated that there would only be four (4) beast kingdom, with the fifth kingdom being the Stone Kingdom of the God of heaven. Thus, it does not matter what form the fourth kingdom takes, or however many diversities of the fourth kingdoms arise, in God's math, there will only be four (4) kingdoms or a combination of all four beast kingdoms. The fifth Kingdom is the Kingdom of God established by people who will rise through Jesus Christ.

[7] Daniel 2:36-45; Daniel 7:15-28

[8] The book of Revelation was probably written between 81 A.D. to 95 A.D.)

[9] Revelation 17:8-11

[10] Daniel 7:12

[11] Daniel 2:36-44, Daniel 7:17;

[12] Daniel 2:44-45; Daniel 7:27

[13] Daniel 7

[14] The lion beast/lion mouth may also represent Mystery Babylon identified in the book of Revelation, also known as the "great city."

[15] Hosea 13:7-8; Hosea 5:14

[16] I was in a season of fasting. It was about the 9th day of the fast in 1992, and it was my first fast going this long. My body was without strength; as I rested on the sofa, and I saw in a trance, and heard a voice say, **"The way is being made for the spirit of Greece."** I then heard a voice say, **"A great tragedy shall happen in America,"** as I heard the voice speak, **I saw a president standing upon a pile of rubble exactly as President Bush did after 9/11.** I then heard the voice say, **"After the tragedy, I will bring forth the Boy Scouts."**

[17] Daniel 10 through Daniel 11

[18] Compare Acts 10:9-10

[19] Revelation 15:2

[20] Strong's Concordance #1063

[21] Acts 17:29 w/Revelation 13:16

[22] Revelation 13:17

[23] Revelation 14:11

[24] Revelation 13:17

[25] Colossians 1:15

[26] John 14:9

[27] Revelation 13:15

[28] Exodus 20:3-5

[29] Exodus 20:5

[30] Revelation 13:15

[31] Revelation 13:8; Revelation 14:12 w/Revelation 14:9-12

[32] Revelation 14:12, Galatians 2:20

[33] 1 Corinthians 10:20

[34] "Charagma," from "charasso" the same root for "character," and is akin to "character" (Vines Expository Dictionary)

[35] "Charakter," from "charasso" the same root for "charagma," and is "akin" to "charagma" (Vines Expository Dictionary)

[36] Romans 11:32-36

[37] Matthew 9:4, Matthew 12:25, Acts 17:29, Hebrews 4:12

[38] Daniel 3

[39] Daniel 8:21-24; Daniel 11:37

[40] 2 Thessalonians 2

[41] Revelation 17; Revelation 13

[42] Note: with respect to homosexuality and lesbianism, it is considered that there are some who practice same-sexuality due to rape, incest, molestation, initiation, and so on. Thus, I believe that God who knows the heart of all, and the reason for all actions, handles each person considering his/her circumstances; even as Jesus' example towards "catamites." In other words, there appears to be two categories of same-sexuality. Those, who God gives over to the practice of same-sexuality for worshipping created things, rather than worshipping the Creator, etcetera; and the other category of those who practice-same-sexuality as a result of incest, rape, molestation, involuntary catamites, and so on.

[43] Revelation 13:2-4; Luke 4:5-8

[44] Romans 1:25; Romans 1:23

[45] "Aschémosuné" ["aschémon + sun" (disfigured-togetherness, shameful-togetherness, deformed-togetherness)]

[46] Revelation 16:13-16

[47] Revelation 16:13; Revelation 19:20 w/Revelation 13:13

[48] Revelation 13:11

[49] 1 John 4:1-3

[50] 1 John 4:5-7 w/Revelation 13:11-18

[51] Revelation 13:16-17

[52] 1 John 5:1

[53] John 1:29

[54] Jude 1:23, Jing James Version

[55] Romans 5:16-19
[56] Matthew 3:11
[57] 2 Chronicles 4:2-6
[58] Exodus 14 and Exodus 15
[59] John 9:1-7
[60] 2 Chronicles 4:4, Philippians 3:13
[61] 2 Chronicle 4:1-6
[62] Job 38:38
[63] 2 Chronicle 4:6
[64] 1 Peter 2:9, Revelation 5:9-10
[65] The Hebrew word for "Red" in the phrase "Red Sea" is "suph" and it also means "end" or "termination" "reed" (Strong's Concordance #5488, #5498, #5490, #5491)
[66] 600 is part of the number of the beast 600-60-6.
[67] Ephesians 4:11-13
[68] Ephesians 6:12
[69] Revelation 17:9-10
[70] Revelation 17:6
[71] Revelation 11:15
[72] " head, the "seventh king"-beast, may represent a period of relative rest for the Saints from State-sponsored persecution.
[73] After Adam and Eve ate from the tree of the knowledge of Good and Evil, they produced in themselves the ability to produce good (including good children) and evil (including evil children)
[74] Genesis 3:15
[75] Matthew 12:34; Matthew 3:7, John 8:44
[76] Matthew 13:38
[77] John 6:70
[78] Luke 22:3; John 13
[79] Revelation 13:15
[80] Compare Deuteronomy 13:1-5
[81] 2 Thessalonians 2, Matthew 7:15-23, Matthew 23:27-29, Matthew 13:41, 2 Peter 2:7
[82] Compare the "prince of Greece" in Daniel 10 that battled with the angel, Gabriel, another angel, Michael, "one of the chief princes" (an archangel)
[83] Daniel 8:21
[84] Revelation 17:12

[85] The "spirit of Greece" can point to the principles and belief of the Greek culture dominating the world again as it did in the days of Alexander, the great, and after Alexander died. Will democracy, as we know it today, be changed to become a war-like imperialistic democracy conquering the world in the same spirit of Alexander?

[86] Antichrist is the false prophet or the spirit, called the false prophet, not the beast—see 1 John 2, 1 John 4

[87] Colossians 1:16

[88] Compare Romans 10:7, where it is clear that the abyss is the place of death

[89] Daniel 10:20

[90] Revelation 16:13-14

[91] Daniel 10

[92] Daniel 8

[93] Revelation 13, Daniel 7

[94] Revelation 17

[95] Revelation 16

[96] Revelation 13:2

[97] Isaiah 2:1-4

[98] Revelation 17:18

[99] Revelation 17:16-17

[100] Daniel 11:36; Revelation 17:16-18

[101] Revelation 17:11

[102] What I saw in 1992 was a president of the United State standing on a heap of rubble as I heard the voice of the Spirit saying to me that "a great tragedy will happen in America." This was the event of 9/11, and it was also fulfilled when President Bush visited New York and stood at Ground Zero.

[103] Homosexuality was common in Greece and Rome as a method of birth control and pleasure. They also used young slave boys for these purposes.

[104] Daniel 8: 21-23

OTHER BOOKS

Poiema, by Judith Peart
Wisdom from Above, by Judith Peart
Procreation, Understanding Sex, and Identity, by Judith Peart
100 Nevers, by Judith Peart
The Shattered and the Healing by Judith Peart
The Lamb, by Donald Peart
Jesus' Resurrection, Our Inheritance, by Donald Peart.
Sexuality, By Donald Peart
Forgiven 490 Times, by Donald Peart w/Judith Peart!
The Days of the Seventh Angel, By Donald Peart
The Torah (The Principle) of Giving, by Donald Peart
The Time Came, by Donald Peart
The Last Hour, the First Hour, the Forty-Second Generation, by Donald Peart
Vision Real, by Donald Peart
The False Prophet, Alias, Another Beast V1, by Donald Peart
"the beast," by Donald Peart
Son of Man Prophesy Against the false prophet, by Donald Peart
The Dragon's Tail, the Prophets Who Teaches Lies, by Donald Peart
The Work of Lawlessness Revealed, by Donald Peart
When the Lord Made the Tempter, by Donald Peart
Examining Doctrine, Volume 1, by Donald Peart
Exousia, Your God Given Authority, by Donald Peart
The Numbers of God, by Donald Peart
The Completions of the Ages … by Donald Peart
The Revelation of Jesus Christ, by Donald Peart
Jude—Translation and Commentary, by Donald Peart
Obtaining the Better Resurrection, by Donald Peart
Manifestations from Our Lord Jesus ...by Donald and Judith Peart
The New Testament, Dr. Donald Peart Exegesis
The Tree of Life, By Dr. Donald Peart
The Spirit and Power of John, the Baptist by Dr. Donald Peart
The Shattered and the Healing by Judith Peart
Is She Married to a Husband? by Donald Peart
The Ugliest Man God Made by Donald Peart
Does Answering the Call of God Impact Your Children? by Donald Peart

Victory Out-of-the Beast-the Harvest of the Earth
Melchizedek, by Donald Peart
Ezekiel-the House-the Land-the City (Interpreting the Patterns), by Donald Peart
Butter and Honey, Understanding how to Choose the Good and Refuse Evil, by Donald Peart

CONTACT INFORMATION:
Crown of Glory Ministries
P.O. Box 1041
Randallstown, MD 21133;
donaldpeart7@gmail.com

ABOUT THE AUTHOR:
Donald Peart is married to Judith Peart since 1986. They believe that Jesus is the Christ, the Son of the living God; and they preach the gospel of God's kingdom centered on Jesus Christ. They have founded and currently oversee Crown of Glory Ministries in Randallstown, Maryland. Donald and his wife have written over 35 books; and their ministry has distributed their books to at least 29 States in the USA and 21 countries. Donald has earned an Associate of Arts degree in Pre-Engineering, a Bachelor of Science degree in Civil Engineering. He also earned a Master of Divinity, a Master of Science in Construction Management, and a Doctorate in Theology.